ECHOES OF FAITH

ECHOES OF FAITH

STORIES WRITTEN IN SPIRIT

NATASHA BARSHALOM

CONTENTS

The book's key takeaway is that healing is a collective journey rooted in acknowledging our individual and shared traumas. Though our life experiences differ, they often reveal common threads of struggle, resilience, and growth. By embracing our vulnerabilities and recognizing the traumas that shape us, we can build stronger, more authentic relationships. These connections create a space where healing becomes possible as we learn from each other's stories and experiences.

The inclusion of journal entries deepens this message by offering personal reflections that allow readers to see the raw, lived experiences behind the lessons. These entries highlight how, despite our differences, we all have the capacity to grow and heal by connecting with others. Sharing these moments encourages readers to look inward, reflect on their own journey, and recognize that healing doesn't have to be a solitary process. It is through relationship building and collective acknowledgment of trauma that we find the strength to heal together.

Triggered Futures, an interactive biography of Natasha Barshalom, hoping to create a wave of collective healing!

BORN BETWEEN TWO WORLDS

I was born on May 26, 1988, in Van Nuys, California, the firstborn to David White and Darlene Butcher. My parents were an unusual pairing, to say the least. My dad, David, grew up in a world of struggle, raised by a runaway from the South who married a Mexican man. Together, they managed apartment buildings across North Hollywood. They weren't wealthy, but they were survivors, resilient in a city that was anything but kind to the vulnerable. My grandmother had a fierce love for people and community. Her heart was for the poor and less fortunate. She was a woman who saw the world for what it was, and that shaped my father in a way that left deep scars.

My dad's father died by suicide—a dark story involving Russian Roulette that haunted his childhood. My dad was just a boy left to wrestle with that trauma, and when my grandmother remarried, things didn't get any easier for him. His stepfather was abusive, both physically and emotionally, and my dad suffered silently. He experienced things that no child should ever endure, including rape.

It wasn't something we talked about often, but I always felt my dad's pain. It lingered in the quiet moments, in the way he would withdraw into himself, and in the way he loved. He was the middle child, caught between an older brother who escaped into the military and a younger brother who fell into the street life of gangbanging and drugs, swept up in the chaos of the '70s and '80s in Los Angeles.

I saw my dad as a man who was trying to make sense of a world that had broken him, yet he loved fiercely. His heart was wide open, even when it was hurting. Maybe that's why my mom fell in love with him so easily.

My mom, Darlene, came from a completely different world —a world of wealth, show business, and family gatherings that felt more like a Hollywood gala than regular Sunday barbecues. She was raised around money and glamour, but she never bought into the illusion.

She knew firsthand the lies and manipulation that came with chasing fame and fortune, and she didn't want any part of it. When she met my dad, the boy from the wrong side of the tracks, she saw something real in him, something pure. Maybe it was his vulnerability or the way he wanted more from life but wasn't sure how to get it.

My mom always saw beyond his pain. She loved him unconditionally, not for where he came from, but for the man she knew he could become. They were both running from something—my dad from the pain of his past, and my mom from the falseness of her world. But together they built something real. Their love was constant even in the midst of hardship, even when it seemed they were at war with themselves. I came into this world already feeling the tension between those two very different lives.

My sister, Felicia, was born in 1991, and while she was all bright smiles, laughter, and energy, I was more like Dad—serious, observant, always trying to fix things even when they weren't mine to fix. Felicia loved to perform, just like the family she was born into, while I was again more withdrawn, trying to make sense of a world that never felt quite steady.

My earliest memories are of family gatherings, big, lively events with both sides of the family, filled with food, laughter, and the smell of barbecues. My grandparents, cousins, and aunts and uncles were always around, but my memories of my own parents are less vivid. It was like they were always in the background, living in a world of their own, while my sister and I soaked up the energy of everyone else—my grandparents, especially on my dad's side, filled the gaps.

Then, in 1994, everything changed. We left California and moved to Las Vegas. My grandfather, Jimmy Caesar, who was an entertainer, had been offered the opening act at the Debbie Reynolds Hotel. My grandparents were showbiz people. My grandma had been a model and jazz singer, and my grandpa was a comedian who had impersonated Frank Sinatra—and let's just say he blew up. Rich and glamorous, sure, but for me, leaving California felt like a betrayal. I had been so close to my dad's family, to that side of myself, and Vegas felt like an entirely different planet. Moving to Vegas wasn't just about leaving behind the physical space of California; it was leaving behind a part of who I was—the pace, the people, everything.

It didn't take long for the dynamic in my family to shift. There was an unspoken tension, a layer of animosity and fear of the unknown. We were suddenly more entrenched in my mom's world, surrounded by the energy of wealth, performance, and high expectations. It wasn't long before my mom's sister moved to Vegas too, and that's when I really started to feel the weight of it all.

I was a daddy's girl through and through. Whatever my dad felt, I felt, and I clung to his disconnect like a lifeline. If he didn't like it, neither did I. But of course, I never told him that. I just followed his lead, absorbing his unease about the move and letting it settle deep within me.

WELCOME TO BABYLON

Living in Vegas came with a price. The city, with its flashing lights and relentless pace, seeped into our family, creating a rift I had never felt before. My father, once a steady source of calm and certainty, seemed uneasy in this new environment. It wasn't the city that disturbed him; it was the absence of something deeper, something familiar. It was as if the love he had once received from his community and, perhaps more importantly, from my mother, became more vivid in its absence than in its presence. He remembered the pain because it was easier than holding on to love that felt distant, intangible.

My mother struggled too. Despite being physically closer to her side of the family, the connection she so desperately needed remained elusive. New beginnings and new opportunities in Vegas didn't erase the absence of those who mattered most. Her family was here, but they might as well have been miles away. My parents had always emphasized the importance of family, and the words "I love you" were often said—but sometimes words are not enough. Love wasn't felt, at least not in the way they needed. Hearts were wide open, but the embrace was cold.

I was growing into my own person during this time, and the fractures in our family were shaping every aspect of my perspective. I could see my mom hurting in ways that I didn't fully understand yet but knew would leave scars. Her relationship with her sister—the one they both shared through their parents—was strained. My mom's oldest sister had a different father, and this division was always made clear, whether intentionally or not. My mother, who leaned heavily on her sister for love and support, was often left feeling inadequate.

Their childhood couldn't have been easy, growing up with grandparents who were too busy performing, lost in their own world. My father, in his quiet way, tried to reassure my mother, bringing her flowers as a gesture of love, reminding her she was cherished. But even those small, tender moments weren't enough to mend the growing distance between them. Vegas wasn't the city of dreams for us; it was a place where we were reminded of all the things we couldn't hold on to.

HIGH SCHOOL AND THE FLASH OF VEGAS

I was 14, getting ready for high school in the late '90s, early 2000s, and everything felt like it was moving too fast. One minute, I was in California, and the next, I was in Las Vegas, standing at the threshold of Cheyenne High School. It felt surreal—like I had just blinked, and suddenly, my childhood was slipping away. The world around me was changing rapidly, especially the media. It was everywhere, growing, influencing, and shaping the way we saw everything. I could sense how powerful it was becoming, even at that age.

At the same time, there was so much going on at home. My grandma in California was getting sick, and all I could think about was how much I wanted to go to Ulysses Grant High School, where my parents had gone. I had heard so many stories about their time there—the friendships, the struggles—it was like a legend in our family. But that wasn't in the cards for me. Instead, I was in Vegas, starting a new chapter with all these emotions and expectations swirling around in my head—some were mine, but most were attached to the dreams and pressures of my parents. I was barely old enough to understand them all.

I had always been well-liked by everyone, but I was never one to have tons of close friends. My sister had always been that one person for me, the person I could lean on no matter what. We had shared so much growing up, so when I started high school and she wasn't there with me, it felt strange, almost like a part of me was missing. She was my anchor in this sea of expectations, and without her, I had to navigate it all on my own.

Ninth grade at Cheyenne High School. I remember taking the public bus every day, passing through the west side of Las Vegas—a place with its own reputation. It was known for being tough, rough around the edges, but to me, it felt like community in a way I hadn't experienced before. Or maybe I was just trying to convince myself of that, to find something familiar in the midst of all the flashing lights of Vegas that seemed to drown out everything else. It was hard to tell what felt like home anymore. I thought back to my childhood and my grandmothers' houses in California. Both were so different, yet both sides of the family provided a sense of community that Vegas seemed to lack.

Cheyenne High School had a reputation too. It was known for fights, gangs, and a whole lot of painful stuff. But even with all that, I met some really incredible people. For the first time, I started to get a clearer sense of who I was and who I wanted to be. Maybe at that time, it didn't feel as deep as it does now, writing this, but I knew I was stepping into something bigger. I was carrying the weight of my parents' pain with me into high school, and without realizing it, I had made up my mind to transform that pain into something meaningful.

High school in Vegas during the 2000s was an experience like no other. Unless you were there, it's hard to explain. The energy of the city bled into everything, and it wasn't just about going to class and doing homework—it was survival. Vegas had this way of shining so bright it could blind you if you weren't careful, and you had to find your way through it all without losing yourself in the flash.

As much as I might drag this out, it's because that time was critical for me. It was a moment of realization, where I began to understand that the world I came from and the world I was stepping into were both shaping me in ways I wasn't ready for. But even in the chaos, I could feel something building within me—a drive, a purpose, even if I couldn't name it yet.

Intermission:

Journal Exercise on Self-Discovery

Caption: "The Importance of Understanding Two Things: Your Why and Your Triggers"

Knowing your "why" reveals who you truly are, while understanding your triggers helps you navigate life through love instead of fear. These two insights are essential for personal growth, and when we take time to reflect on them, we can live more intentionally and authentically.

Journal Entry:

Getting to Know Your Triggers

Triggers are emotional responses that surface when something in our environment touches a past hurt or unresolved issue. By identifying and understanding them, we can choose to work with them, rather than letting them work against us.

1. Identify Your Triggers:

What situations or people make you feel reactive, angry, or upset?

____

____

____

Reflect on past experiences where you felt a strong emotional reaction. What was the common theme?

____

____

____

2. Acknowledge the Feelings:

Write down the emotions you feel when you're triggered. Are you feeling insecure, unloved, or misunderstood?

____

____

____

Be honest with yourself. It's okay to feel uncomfortable emotions—acknowledging them is the first step toward healing.

____

____

____

3. **Explore the Origin:**

Where do these triggers come from? Are they linked to childhood experiences, family dynamics, or past relationships?

____

____

____

Reflect on how past events may have shaped your emotional responses.

____

____

____

4. **Work With Your Triggers**

Next time you feel triggered, pause and take a deep breath. Ask yourself, "What is this really about?"

____

____

____

Instead of reacting impulsively, respond with curiosity. What is the lesson in this trigger? What can it teach you about yourself?

____

____

____

5. Create New Responses

Replace old reactions with new, more loving responses. If you tend to withdraw when triggered, try reaching out and expressing how you feel. If anger is your default, try responding with calm and compassion.

Practice patience. Over time, you will retrain your emotional responses.

Reflection Page: Where Can You Relate?

Take a moment to reflect on areas of your life where you may have experienced triggers or found yourself reacting out of fear instead of love. Use the following prompts to guide your reflection:

- Have you ever reacted strongly to something that, in hindsight, wasn't as significant as it seemed?
- Do you find yourself feeling defensive in certain situations, especially with loved ones or colleagues?
- Can you think of moments where fear of rejection or failure held you back from taking action?

- How does your past influence your present-day reactions? Are there any patterns you notice?

Write down your thoughts and take time to reflect. This is your journey of understanding.

____

____

____

____

____

____

Your Why: A Fun Exercise in Self-Discovery

Knowing your "why" is like having a compass—it helps you navigate life with purpose. This fun exercise will help you uncover your "why" and remind you of the things that make you, you.

6. What Brings You Joy?

Write down five things that light you up, things that make you feel truly happy and alive. These can be simple things like spending time with loved ones, working on a passion project, or being in nature.

____

____

____

7. What Motivates You?

What gets you out of bed in the morning? Is it the desire to make a difference in the world, to provide for your family, or to follow a creative passion? Write down the driving forces in your life.

____

____

____

8. Who Do You Want to Be?

Picture yourself in five years. What kind of person do you want to be? How do you want others to remember you? Write this vision in as much detail as possible.

____

____

____

9. Connect the Dots

Look back at your answers. What themes do you see? How do these answers reflect your values, passions, and purpose? Write a sentence that sums up your "why." This is your guiding principle.

Example: "My why is to inspire others to embrace their authentic selves and lead lives full of love and purpose, because I believe we are all here to uplift and support one another."

____

____

____

Reflection: Your Why

Now that you've completed the exercise, take a moment to reflect:

- How does your why align with your daily actions?
- Are there areas where you can live more intentionally, guided by your why?
- How does knowing your why help you face challenges or fears?

Write down any insights or feelings that come up. This is the heart of your personal journey, and it's an ongoing discovery.

IT'S GETTING HEAVY

Hopefully, that intermission was a breath of fresh air. I haven't mentioned it yet, but journaling has truly been my saving grace. It helps me process when things get heavy, and now, as I look back from where I stand today, I've learned an important truth: we can't hide from the hard stuff. When we face it, that's where we find our strength.

But let's get back to it. I was surrounded by great people, a sense of community that took me right back home—not down the street, but all the way to the valley in California. It felt like a connection to the life I had before Vegas. And it was exciting, even comforting. Not that my mom and dad weren't doing a great job raising us, but Vegas—it took its toll. The pain I always sensed in my parents seemed to take on a different shape: more visible, more intense. Their focus had shifted to providing and nurturing as much as they could, but I could feel something was missing.

My mom and dad were different in a lot of ways, but their differences brought balance. Still, their own deep-rooted pain made it hard to feel the love, even if they said it 500 times a day. I never doubted their love, but love isn't just words—it's felt. And in those years, I struggled to feel it.

On the flip side, the friends I had at school were from neighborhoods known for being "bad areas" of Vegas. But I didn't see that. What I saw were good people—humble, loving people with a deep sense of integrity. They were just living in neighborhoods trapped in a loop, broken by systems that were designed to fail them. Pill mills were everywhere back then; you could sit in a doctor's office like you were waiting for food stamps and walk out with thousands of dollars' worth of pharmaceuticals. And where were these clinics? Right in the heart of poverty, just like where the drugs were being dropped off. The cops were crooked, and only a five-minute walk separated these neighborhoods from the glittering lights of the Strip.

If you've ever flown into Vegas, you've probably seen it— the one blacked-out area right beside the Strip, visible from the sky. That's the west side, and despite its reputation, I loved it there. It had something the rest of Vegas didn't: community. Real community, made up of good people fighting against a crooked system, trying to get out; and when they did, many of them gave back. That community, those people, felt closer to God than anything I'd ever experienced.

And I rebelled to keep that feeling alive. At first, I didn't realize that what I was feeling was shaping my story—this story I'm writing now. But as I reflect on it, it makes me smile because it was real, it was heavy, and it came with a price. Whatever I felt in that environment triggered my dad in ways I couldn't fully grasp back then. He didn't need to whoop me to let me know. His disappointment and disapproval were enough, and it pushed me further into the very thing he wanted to keep me away from—the west side, the community, the friends I made at school, the image of it all.

It triggered my dad because I think, deep down, he saw how much I loved it there. And it wasn't just about the people or the place—it was about him. I loved my dad deeply, and in a strange way, that environment made me feel connected to him, to the man I missed from my childhood. I think part of me was trying to recapture something I felt as a young girl, something I lost along the way.

Both my parents' families became increasingly important to me during this time. It wasn't just because of the people themselves, but because of the love my parents had for them. That love bled into me and my sister. We knew the power of love, and we would do anything to stay in it, to hold onto it, even when it felt distant or strained. The weight of their pain and their love shaped me, and as heavy as it was, it also made me who I am today.

UNVEILING THE PAIN

OK, it's a biography, so I have to tell the deepest, most painful parts because those moments shape everything about who we become, who I became.

It was around 10th grade when my brother was born. Yes, I have a brother, and I truly believe he holds a big purpose in our bloodline—a beautiful boy, a beacon amid everything going on. I stopped going to school after he came, making it easier for Mom and Dad. Let's be honest: the majority of my dad's problems with me were focused on school, so when I dropped out, things quieted down on that front, at least for a while.

But this chapter might hurt my loved ones. It's my truth, and a book about my life wouldn't be complete if I didn't write from my perspective, from my memory. That's all this is—my truth. I love my family deeply, and I don't hold their wrongs against them. Hurt people hurt people, and most of the time, it's not intentional, and there has been forgiveness.

OK, deep breath. I'm gonna grab some water, because this part is where it starts to get heavy.

Memories from my childhood started to surface around this time, memories I had buried. Guilt crept in from things. I didn't understand massages from cousins that honestly didn't feel quite right looks from

uncles that felt inappropriate then, the worse rape by a family member.

It wasn't talked about. It stayed in the dark. And I carried the weight alone growing up as a girl in the 2000s, when sex and the trauma of our parents generation were used against us. It started to feel like a lot.

Maybe all of that had something to do with why I identified as a lesbian for quite some time. I remember flashes of memory touches that didn't sit right—feelings of discomfort from people I was supposed to trust. Writing this is hard, but it's my truth, and letting go of the attached emotional trauma is therapy. That's healing.

When my grandpa Jimmy Cesar, my mom's stepdad, died, it shook everything. His death wasn't just a loss. It shifted the whole dynamic of our family. My mom loved him more than she realized, and losing him unexpectedly. Hit her heart, and all this time my dad had gotten tougher, really tough.

By then I was no longer in school, which I didn't realize was an escape for me; instead, I was with my new baby brother to care for. It was a lot. I always seem to be in trouble already having dealings with the police. Definitely not the future I envisioned for myself as a young child.

Life, our cycles—they come at a price. From birth through childhood, we carry so much hope in faith. We're fearless. Then, as teenagers, we start to feel the pressure of our parents expectations. High school comes, and suddenly we're grappling with our identities, trying to figure out who we are. It was overwhelming.

I know I'm jumping ahead, but I'm sparing you all the little details because this book would be 1000 pages long if I didn't. So, we're fast forwarding to 2009, a pivotal year in my life. But before we get there, remember everything I went through, everything I'm sharing. It's all part of the process of becoming who I am today.

RUNNING INTO THE FIRE

By this time in my life, I was used to pain. Trauma had become a deep, ingrained part of who I was. It was no longer something that happened to me; it was something I carried, something that shaped every part of who I was becoming. 2009 was a pivotal year, but before we dive in, I have to backtrack a little. I had to take a breather from the last chapter—just like back then, I would run or turn the page whenever I felt triggered. But this time, we're telling the truth, so I can't just run. We've got to go back a bit to make sense of where I'm coming from. Part of publishing this book is about overcoming and letting go, so let's go back.

I left home the year I turned 18. Can anyone guess where I ran to? The west side. Back to the place that held a sense of community, the place where my childhood memories began creeping up on me. My mom and dad were hurting, working hard to survive, and my brother had just been born. I thought leaving was the best option—that everyone would be better off without me there.

The west side still had that sense of community, but living there was a whole different story. I didn't come from there, so I had to earn my place. I was an outsider. I didn't belong. So, overnight, I became a different version of myself—a version I hadn't met before. Maybe that's what my dad was trying to protect me from: what it's really like to live in these neighborhoods, the struggle, the grind, and what people go through to develop a mindset that values morals and integrity in a world that often forgets those things.

What did that look like for me? More time in jail, working at different escort services, and surrounding myself with friends who were pimps and working girls. I was just playing the cards I was dealt. It was a lot, but I know I put myself there. And honestly, I don't regret any of it. There were so many days filled with hurt, but I also took away lessons that have become a huge part of the person writing this book right now.

Life is about being present. I had to be present in the midst of all that chaos, and it taught me so much. It wasn't easy, but it was real. And now, as I write these words, I'm realizing how those experiences, those tough lessons, shaped me into who I am today. It was a journey through pain and transformation, one that I don't take lightly. But I'm here now, and I'm telling my story.

Transformation Exercise:

Embracing Change and Growth

Transformation is not just a moment; it's a process. It's about acknowledging where you've been, understanding how it's shaped you, and deciding how you want to move forward. This exercise will guide you through reflecting on your own journey and help you actively embrace the transformation that's happening within you.

Step 1: Acknowledge the Past

Before we can transform, we need to acknowledge the experiences that brought us here. These can be painful moments, lessons learned, or challenges overcome.

Write down a few key experiences that have deeply impacted you. These might be moments of pain, trauma, or hardship. They could also be times when you felt lost or confused, times when you ran from the truth or didn't know how to cope.

____

____

____

Reflection Prompt:

How did these experiences shape who you are today? What

did they teach you about yourself, even if it was hard to accept?

____

____

____

Step 2: Let Go of What No Longer Serves You

Transformation requires us to release what is holding us back, whether it's fear, guilt, shame, or limiting beliefs.

Now, make a list of the things you're ready to let go of. These might be old habits, negative self-talk, toxic relationships, or emotions you've been holding onto for too long.

____

____

____

Reflection Prompt:

What will letting go of these things open up for you? How will it feel to release these burdens?

Step 3: Visualize the New You

Transformation is also about envisioning the person you are becoming. It's about looking ahead with hope and purpose.

Close your eyes and imagine the transformed version of yourself. What does this person look like? How do they feel? How do they carry themselves through life? What are the qualities of this new version of you? Strength? Compassion? Resilience?

Now, write a description of your transformed self. Use present tense, as if you are already living as this version of yourself.

Example:

I am strong and fearless, unafraid to face challenges. I no longer let my past define me; instead, I use it as fuel to grow. I walk with purpose and share my story to inspire others.

____

____

____

____

____

Step 4: Take Action Steps Toward Transformation

Transformation requires action. It's not just about how we think or feel—it's about what we do. What steps can you take, starting today, to move closer to your transformed self?

Write down three actionable steps you can take this week to move closer to the person you're becoming. These steps don't have to be big; they can be small shifts that bring you closer to the life you want.

Example:

- Start journaling daily to reflect on your emotions.
- Practice self-compassion by speaking kindly to yourself.
- Set boundaries with people or situations that no longer align with your transformation.

____

____

____

Step 5: Embrace the Process

Transformation doesn't happen overnight. It's a journey with highs and lows, but every step forward is progress.

Write a mantra or affirmation to remind yourself that you are on the path of transformation.

Example:

"I honor my journey and trust that every step I take brings me closer to my highest self."

____

____

____

Reflection

Now that you've worked through the steps of this exercise, take a moment to reflect:

- How do you feel about the process of transformation?
- What emotions are coming up for you as you

acknowledge your past and look toward your future?

- How will you continue to nurture this transformation in your daily life?

____

____

____

____

____

____

Transformation is about stepping into the fullness of who you are meant to be. Be patient with yourself, and remember that growth takes time. You are exactly where you need to be.

THE YEAR EVERYTHING CHANGED

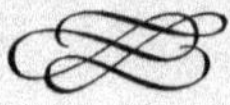

This year was crazy. I was fresh out of a breakup, and that breakup was honestly the catalyst that led me to my first real soul tie—a friendship with Megan and Kapua. And let me tell you, that dynamic was wild. But here's the thing: everything—I mean everything—is already written. We all serve a purpose, and nothing happens by mistake.

Let's get into it.

My friendship with Megan brought me to Kapua, which led to my breakup, making it easy for what happened next to unfold. I had a lot of girlfriends, and none of those relationships felt balanced. It was like I was searching for something, but I didn't know what, and it kept leading me in circles. Long story short, that year I moved in with an ex-girlfriend who had a boyfriend—and that boyfriend had a best friend by the name of Phill Weaver. And yep, that's who I ended up spending the next 14 years with.

But let's not rush—my heart's pounding just thinking about it.

Let's give this story some context.

At the time, I had been couch surfing, and life was getting dark. I had been working as a madam at an escort service, and due to trauma and corruption within that world, I was praying for change. Beaten by pimps for not sending the girls on enough calls, dealing with crooked cops, and witnessing broken homes, I needed a way out. I was praying for love, for something different. I had spent months wandering around the Downtown Las Vegas (DTC) area, just lost in my thoughts, wanting a new path. That's when I was invited to move in with my ex, and I accepted. Sorry if I'm jumping around a bit, but this part of my life was just as chaotic as it sounds.

It was fight night weekend, just a few months after All-Star Weekend in Vegas, when I met Phill. Right away, there was this instant attraction. For me, that was new, because up until then, I was convinced I was a lesbian. But after one night of smoking and talking, we were spending every day together. We spent countless hours on the phone, and slowly, my life began to change. I left the makeup industry and the escort service behind. I was starting to remember what I really wanted out of life: happiness, for myself and for my loved ones.

As the months went by, my thoughts and perspectives deepened. Being with a man felt different but also familiar. It reminded me of the energy I saw between my mom and dad, the balance that comes from building something out of love. There was something about the dynamic of a man and a woman that made me feel grounded in a way I hadn't expected. I was falling in love with Phill.

But then, about seven months in, Phill went to jail. His best friend Brian handed me Phill's belongings, including his phone, so I could stay in touch with him. The next day, an unknown number called, and of course, I answered—I thought it was Phill calling from jail. But no, it was his wife. I froze as she asked why Phill wasn't home at 4 AM, the time he usually got off work. That's when everything shattered. She didn't know he had lost his job at Target, and she had no idea that when he wasn't at home, he was with me.

I was blindsided. Why, God? Why me? I never wanted to be a homewrecker. I would never allow myself to fall in love with a man who had a wife and child—never.

When Phill got out of jail the next day, I confronted him. I handed him his phone, filled with all the evidence I'd uncovered—pictures of his marriage certificate, his daughter. He tried to explain everything, told me they were separated, gave me all these excuses. But all I heard was blah blah blah. I couldn't hear any of it. We broke up, and within two weeks, I moved to Killeen, Texas, to live with another ex-girlfriend.

Yeah, I was kind of a houchie when it came to the ladies back then.

But this chapter of my life? It gets deeper. A lot deeper.

THE CYCLE OF LOVE AND PAIN

Time passed, and I found myself working at a bank in Texas. By then, I had come to terms with two things: love is real, but people, sometimes, are not. It hurt like hell, but it was what it was. As soon as I accepted that, the calls started again. Phill was back in my life, but this time it felt different. There was something heavier in the air—games were being played. We would talk for hours, just like before, but the next day, I'd get a call from his wife.

It hit me hard. I couldn't do this to his wife, to his daughter, or to myself. I blocked my number, trying to make a clean break. No matter how many chapters had passed between then and now, I still felt that way deep down. I would never forget that sense of guilt, the feeling that I had crossed a line I swore I'd never touch.

Then one day, everything shifted again. My ex, Ayreo, who by this time was more like a sister to me, picked me up from work. "Girl, when we get home, you need to get fly," she said with a smirk. "Like sexy fly. We're going to Austin." I was confused, asking, "For what?" but she brushed it off, saying we were going out but that she had to make a quick stop at the airport to pick up a friend.

It was a long drive, nearly two hours to Austin, and when we got there, Ayreo went straight into actress mode. She gave me this whole elaborate story about why I had to go in and wait for her "friend." I stood there at the airport, scanning the crowd for the girl she described, but instead, I saw Phill. Coming down the escalator. He dropped his bags and ran to me.

Everything in me froze. I felt an overwhelming amount of love, but I was also taken aback by his first words: "I choose you."

The ride to the club that night was awkward. There was so much unspoken pain between us, but I pushed it aside. I ignored the reality of his daughter, his seven-year relationship that he had walked away from, and all the damage that came with it. Ayreo had her own friends to meet, so it was just the three of us hanging out, pretending like everything was fine. I buried the hurt deep and fell right back into the familiar feeling of missing him.

But the days that followed were heavy with lingering doubt. And then, everything fell apart.

I snapped at work one day. The pressure, the emotions, everything just built up, and I lost my job. Out of fear, I went straight back to old habits—stealing, just to survive. It was a mistake I would regret deeply, because I got caught. Before I knew it, I was sitting in a jail cell in Killeen, Texas.

Those three days in jail were a wake-up call for me. I was terrified, and it scared me straight. Ever since then, I've stayed far away from anything criminal. But during those three days, Phill and I barely spoke. We had talked a bit, but obviously, jail isn't the place for long conversations.

When I got out on bail, I headed back to the house. Just as I arrived, Phill was on his way out—to the airport. He had made plans to go back to Vegas. I didn't know it at the time, but his child's mother was a travel agent. Booking a flight for him was easy, and while I was sitting in jail, he was making plans to leave.

But here's the thing—he didn't go. He didn't know I was getting out of jail that day, and I didn't know I would be released after only three days. Killeen, being a military base, has a unique setup for civilian offenders, and they set bail for you automatically. After three days, they transfer you to another county for court. I was released without even knowing it was coming.

At that moment, I told myself it was a sign—we were meant to be. And I ran with that thought. I ran with it, even though deep down I knew that nothing about this situation was simple or easy. I convinced myself that everything was happening for a reason, that all the chaos and pain was leading me toward something greater.

But in reality, it was just the beginning of another chapter in a long, complicated story—a story I was still figuring out how to navigate.

BACK TO VEGAS

It didn't take long for things to get complicated in Texas. My friend had a huge heart, and an even bigger family, and her home filled up quickly with people who needed a place to stay. She was the backbone for so many, but with so many people coming and going, it was time for me to move on. So, I went back to Vegas—something I was terrified of. It felt like I was walking into an episode of *Baby Boy*—any time I wasn't around, Phill would be with his wife. Yes, he was still married.

My spirit knew this was wrong. I was raised to understand love and the sanctity of marriage, especially in the eyes of God. Nothing about this could end well. But my mind kept telling me something different: "This is meant for you. There's no loyalty between you and this other woman." I paid a heavy price for that mindset.

Through the lessons of my mistakes, I started to realize that life wasn't just about right and wrong—it was about being centered, being able to differentiate between what my spirit knew and what my flesh wanted. This is when I began paying attention. It felt like my life had become a movie— or maybe it was all of us, with technology creating a shift in our environment. Everything was fast, intense, and out of control, like we were living in a scene from one of our favorite movies, *Baby Boy.* Why was it that way? When you acknowledge the truth behind that question, it's the result of pain, trauma, and the struggles we all go through. But when you come from broken cities, poverty, and the weight of systemic oppression, it gets heavy real fast.

Phill and I knew our relationship was wrong in so many ways, but we found common ground in how we supported each other through our trauma. Phill was born in Watts, California, in 1980, and he grew up feeling the direct impact of the Rodney King beating and the Watts riots. He witnessed the crack epidemic up close, the devastation it caused, and the way it shaped his community. But it was also those very circumstances that made it easy for me to fall in love with him.

Just like my mom did with my dad, I fell for a young man from the other side of the tracks. Phill reminded me of my father—he was a fly D-Boy, straight out of California, with swagger. But beyond all that, Phill was still the little boy who knew God, the one who loved his mom unconditionally, even though she was one of his deepest wounds. He carried forgiveness for the father who was never there, and he deeply respected his older brother, a shot caller in the hood who had become a role model of leadership for him.

Phill was kind, loving, and pure at heart, but like my dad, he was a man trying to hold on to the feeling of love that you only experience as a child. I quickly realized that I was on a path toward my purpose, a path that looked so familiar to so many of us. Circumstances had placed me in a role of observation, and I knew I had to give it all to God.

Three years passed in the blink of an eye. We spent those years going back and forth, grappling with the triggers of family, love, and the dynamics of being in Vegas. Time flew by, and honestly, the memories from those years are a blur. It was a whirlwind of emotions, mistakes, and realizations, but through it all, I felt like I was being guided toward something greater.

The relationship, the pain, the lessons—they all played a role in shaping me. And though it was difficult, I knew deep down that every experience, every heartache, was leading me closer to my purpose.

THE MOVE TO DENVER AND THE SHIFTING WORLD

By the time 2012 was approaching, it felt like the world was on the verge of change—not just for me but for everyone. The media had fully leaned into fear tactics, constantly pushing scarcity and uncertainty. 9/11 had already happened, and there was this constant buzz about the world coming to an end in 2012. In a way, looking back, that world did end—energetically, at least. It was a time when everything felt like it was shifting, including my family.

Somehow, we ended up in Denver, Colorado. My mom, in true form, was calling me constantly, with her dramatic take on what was to come as we entered 2012. You guessed it—Phill moved to Colorado too, and we found ourselves living with my parents, brother, and sister in Thornton. The dynamic was anything but easy. Phill and I had been rocky for a while, and moving in with my family only magnified the tensions.

Phill was a very active dad in his daughter's life, and leaving her behind to move to Colorado wasn't easy for him. He loved her deeply, and honestly, I knew that he still had feelings for his wife. They had spent seven years together, after all, and she had given him his first daughter. I told myself that I gave him a choice—either stay with his family or come with me—but in reality, I was trying to protect his image. I saw how much he loved them both, and I knew deep down that part of him was still tied to them.

Our relationship was anything but stable. I convinced myself that we could make it work, but I was constantly struggling with the reality of what I knew. Phill loved his wife, and she was beautiful, as expected. She had been with him through so much, and he was a good man at heart— just like my dad. But that's where things got complicated. Phill and my dad shared a lot of similar traumas, which meant they also had common triggers. Let me paint you a picture—yes, there were moments where my dad and Phill almost got physical, and that was terrifying for me. It's hard to see the two men you care about so deeply getting that close to a fight, but somehow, we worked through it.

After almost a year of living with my family, we finally found jobs and saved enough money to get our own place. We moved to Aurora, Colorado, into a small studio apartment. We were paying $700 a month, and for a while, life seemed great. We had our own space, we were making money, and from the outside, things looked like they were finally falling into place. But the more we had, the deeper Phill's pain became.

He was still holding onto the love he felt for his daughter, the guilt of leaving her behind, and the memories of the people who gave him a sense of community during his darkest days. On top of that, Phill carried even more guilt because he wasn't just absent from his daughter's life—he also had a son from another relationship. Another amazing woman. And he hadn't been there for his son either.

This guilt started eating away at him. The drinking started to drown his emotions, and it took a toll on us. My dad had never turned to substances to cope with his pain, but Phill was different. While their emotions were similar, their ways of handling them were not. Phill's drinking created a chasm between us, and it began to feel like we were falling apart.

The weight of his past, the unresolved guilt, and the deep love he still had for his children were pulling him in different directions. And while I wanted to be there for him, I realized that I was part of the problem, too. I wasn't just living my story; I was living his pain, his guilt, and the mistakes of both our pasts.

We thought we had made it when we moved into that little apartment, but really, the cracks in our foundation were just becoming more visible. We were both searching for happiness, but instead, we found the ghosts of our pasts lurking in every corner of that studio.

Journal Entry: Acknowledging Patterns Attached to Trauma

Today, I want to focus on recognizing the patterns in my life that are deeply connected to my trauma. I've spent so much time pushing through the pain, trying to move forward, that I often forget to step back and see the patterns that keep repeating. These patterns, though difficult to acknowledge, are rooted in the traumas I've experienced, and until I confront them fully, they will continue to shape my choices and reactions.

Reflection: Recognizing the Patterns

What are the recurring themes in my life?

I keep finding myself in relationships where I'm the one holding on, even when I know it's not healthy. I see it now, in Phill, and even in past relationships with women. There's always this deep need for love, yet I choose partners who are emotionally unavailable or tied to something—or someone—else.

How does this tie back to my trauma?

I think part of this comes from my childhood, where I always felt like I had to earn love. Whether it was with my parents, dealing with their own struggles, or the unresolved feelings of guilt and shame from being violated by people who should've protected me, I learned early that love felt conditional. These traumas made me believe that I had to work for love, even when it hurt me.

What emotions come up when I think about this?

Guilt, shame, frustration—but also a sense of clarity. Seeing the pattern helps me understand why I make the choices I do, but it also brings up the fear of breaking free from it. Can I love without attaching myself to pain? That's the question I have to answer.

Exercises: Breaking the Patterns

1. Identifying the Source of the Pattern

Exercise: Write down one recurring pattern in your life, something that consistently brings you pain or keeps you stuck in unhealthy cycles.

Prompt: "One recurring pattern in my life is _______."

Next, think about where this pattern might have started. Was it from a childhood experience, a significant relationship, or even a belief you adopted over time?

Prompt: "I believe this pattern started when _______."

Example:

One recurring pattern in my life is chasing emotionally unavailable people.

I believe this pattern started when I felt like I had to earn love from my parents, who were often emotionally distant, focused on their own struggles.

____

____

____

____

____

2. Reframing the Narrative

Exercise: Now that you've identified the pattern and its origin, let's reframe the narrative. How can you look at this pattern differently, as something you have the power to change?

Prompt: "Instead of continuing this pattern, I will choose to ________."

Example:

Instead of continuing this pattern, I will choose to seek relationships where I am loved and valued without conditions. I will no longer hold on to people who cannot fully be present in my life.

____

____

____

____

____

3. Practicing Self-Compassion

Exercise: Trauma can make us hard on ourselves, especially when we see the same mistakes over and over. It's important to practice self-compassion as we work through these patterns.

Prompt: Write a compassionate letter to yourself, acknowledging the hurt you've carried and the strength it takes to face these patterns.

Example:

Dear self, I see the pain you've carried for so long, and I understand why it's been so hard to break free. You've been hurt by people you loved and trusted, and that's left a deep wound. But you are not defined by your past. You are strong, you are capable, and you are worthy of love—real love. It's okay to make mistakes; what matters is that you're trying to grow. I'm proud of you for that.

____

____

____

____

____

4. Mindful Decision-Making

Exercise: The next time you find yourself repeating a pattern, take a moment to pause and ask yourself, "Is this a reaction based on my past trauma, or am I making this choice from a place of love and healing?"

Action Step: Practice this mindfulness exercise during a triggering moment and journal afterward about what came up for you.

Example:

Today, I caught myself falling back into the pattern of over-explaining myself in a conversation, afraid I wasn't being understood or accepted. I paused and realized this was rooted in my childhood experiences of feeling unheard. Instead of spiraling, I took a deep breath and reminded myself that I don't need to prove my worth to anyone. That was a big step.

____

____

____

____

____

Reflection: Where Do I Go From Here?

Now that I've identified my patterns, reframed them, and begun practicing mindfulness, where do I go from here? This is the part of the journey where I actively choose to break free from the cycle.

Journal Prompt: What can I do today to nurture a new, healthy pattern in my life?

Example: "I will start by setting clear boundaries in my relationships, saying no to situations that compromise my emotional well-being, and reminding myself that I am worthy of unconditional love."

____

____

____

____

____

Final Thoughts:

The patterns we fall into are not our fault, but breaking them is our responsibility. It's not easy, but acknowledging them is the first step toward healing and growth. Today, I commit to being aware of my patterns, showing compassion to myself when they surface, and making conscious choices to live in alignment with love, not trauma.

A STEADY PACE, A HEALING HEART

It was mid-2016, and for the first time in what felt like forever, my life had found some sense of balance. Looking back now, it's strange to think that in the midst of yet another loss, I felt steadier. Yes, I had lost another pregnancy — another gut-wrenching chapter in my journey of motherhood that I thought would break me. But instead, I found strength where I thought only pain would exist.

Somehow, amidst it all, life had started to move forward in ways I hadn't expected.

Phillip's daughter visited us in Denver that summer, and for almost a month, it felt like we were a family. Seeing Phillip with his daughter, the pure joy she brought him, filled me with both happiness and a familiar pang of guilt. His love for her was undeniable, and while it was beautiful to witness, it stirred those complicated feelings in me —

the kind that were tied to his struggles with loyalty and my own longings for what we didn't yet have. But in those moments, watching him be a father, I saw how deeply he cared and how much he had healed too.

That summer wasn't just about external changes; there was a profound internal shift happening in me. Over the past year and a half, I had lost almost 150 pounds. It wasn't some miracle diet or a fleeting trend. It was the result of accountability — learning portion control, cutting out sugar and carbs, staying active. I didn't allow myself the comfort of excuses anymore. Instead, I took charge, and with each pound lost, I felt lighter, not just in body but in spirit. It was as though I was shedding the grief and loss I had carried with me for so long.

Phillip and I were climbing the ladder in our careers too, bringing in more income, which felt like an external validation of the progress we were making internally. It's funny how, when one part of your life starts to align, everything else begins to follow. Yet, despite the growth and success, there were still parts of us — parts of me — that hadn't fully healed. My family had moved to Idaho, and while it was a positive move for them, it brought up old wounds for my mom. I could see the pain in her eyes, the weight of unresolved grief she still carried from losing her mother and the lingering void left by her sister. The echoes of loss were never far behind.

But something else shifted that year. As I was healing physically, emotionally, and spiritually, new relationships began to blossom One of the most important ones was with my godchildren — Tutu, Amir, Jojo, and Khalia. Those babies, with their wide-eyed wonder and boundless energy, became a source of healing I never knew I needed. Their innocence, their fearlessness, the way they approached life with open hearts filled a part of me that had been broken for so long. They didn't erase my fertility struggles, but they gave me a new perspective, a new way to hold that pain without letting it consume me.

Every moment spent with them was a reminder of the beauty that still existed in the world. They brought laughter into my home, joy into my heart, and a sense of purpose that extended beyond the struggles of my past. Watching them grow, seeing their curiosity unfold, was like seeing the world through fresh eyes — untainted, hopeful, and full of potential. They reminded me of God's presence in the most ordinary of moments, in the simplicity of play, in the sound of their laughter.

Their innocence healed parts of me that I thought were irreparably broken. They taught me that life doesn't have to be perfect to be beautiful. That sometimes, healing comes not in the way we expect but in the form of small hands holding yours or in the sound of children's laughter filling the room.

These children, with their boundless energy and fearless spirits, brought me back to life in ways I hadn't realized I needed.

Being around them, I found myself present in a way I hadn't been before — soaking in the moments, being grateful for the now, and finding peace in the simplicity of life. They motivated me to be a better person, to continue healing, and to appreciate the journey I was on. And maybe, through them, I started to believe that everything would, in fact, be okay.

THRIVING THROUGH THE DIVES

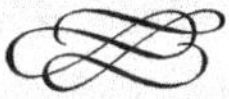

Work was booming. I was thriving at the tour operation company, enjoying all the perks that came with it, including the possibility of traveling internationally. My boss had plans to take me to either Colombia or Costa Rica, and just the thought of it was surreal. At the same time, life at home was shifting. Things at our apartment were chaotic, but Phillip and I were preparing for something big—moving into our first home together. It wasn't as homeowners, but still, a four-bedroom house in Aurora felt like a major step for us. We had a few months to wait before moving in, so we stayed with Coolen, a close friend and the mother of two of my godchildren. Living with her wasn't just about finding a place to stay; it felt like spending more time with family.

I started working part-time at Five Guys, where Coolen was the general manager. It was fun, a welcome distraction, but deeper changes were happening within me. The weight loss had transformed more than just my body —it had shifted my entire mindset. For the first time in my relationship with Phillip, I found myself noticing other people. Not in a way that crossed any lines, but it scared me to even entertain the thoughts. I wondered, why now? Why was I feeling this way?

The weight loss had done more than change how I looked; it changed how I saw myself and my life. I realized that life was what we made of it, and while not all of my trauma was my fault, I still played a role in how I let it shape me. Meanwhile, Phillip wasn't healing. The more I grew, the more I noticed his pain deepening. I never thought I was better than him, but it was hard not to see that his drinking was taking a toll. Over the years, our relationship had slipped into a routine. We weren't living—we were surviving, weighed down by the unresolved trauma we both carried.

As the year went on, something unexpected happened. I developed feelings for a mutual friend—someone who had been in our lives for years, someone who knew all the ins and outs of my relationship with Phillip. The feelings weren't one-sided; they were mutual. And although we never acted on them, acknowledging the emotions was enough to stir up guilt, shame, and confusion. Change has a way of bringing everything to the surface—memories, fears, and the instinct to protect ourselves.

By the end of the year, I found myself pregnant again—my sixth pregnancy. This one made it to 21 weeks before I lost it. It felt like my body was stuck in a routine, like it had been programmed to fail.

Just like my mind, programmed by years of trauma, loss, and survival.

FROM ASHES TO HOPE

It felt like a slow unraveling, like a thread pulled too tight until it snaps. I didn't see it coming, not fully. How could I, when life was so wrapped in the chaos of survival, of holding everything together for everyone else? But this year was different. This was the year that everything broke apart—not in some gentle unraveling, but in a violent crash that left me exposed to the harsh light of reality.

Phill's son had come to visit, and within months, he moved in. Our house, once a refuge, now felt crowded, suffocating under the weight of unresolved trauma. My family moved in too, after losing my grandmothers. It was like they were chasing something—perhaps love, perhaps closure, or maybe just each other. But whatever it was, it was slipping through their fingers. Dad's health began to deteriorate quickly; oxygen tanks became part of our daily scenery. Mom was sinking into the haze of pain medication, her fibromyalgia diagnosis only adding to the void that was growing between us. Felicia, my sister, was battling her own demons, even overdosing in the midst of it all. The house was no longer a home; it was a storm gathering force.

And there I was, in the eye of it, trying to balance everything, trying to keep things together when all I wanted to do was run. Each drive home from work became harder. I could feel the knot in my stomach tightening the closer I got to the house, knowing the fights with Phill were inevitable. The drinking, the shouting, the triggers for my father, my mother slipping away into her own world—and me? I was sinking too.

Phill's son, Jr., was lost. He paced the house, desperate for his father's attention, but Phill was drowning in his own unresolved pain. I tried to fill the void, but my efforts only made the weight heavier. I was suffocating under the constant demands of everyone needing something from me—my parents, my sister, Phill, Jr. My own brother, confused and distant, saw Jr. as competition for my affection. I was stuck in a constant tug-of-war, and no matter what I did, it felt like I was failing everyone.

The pressure was unbearable. I had lost myself, even though I had shed so much—weight, trauma, pain. But the more I shed, the more that old, festering pain came to the surface, forcing me to confront it. And I couldn't—not when everyone around me was breaking. I wanted to scream. I wanted to rage. And eventually, I did.

I let it consume me. I let it take over, this rage. It wasn't just anger; it was a violent storm of frustration, guilt, and helplessness. Nights were spent yelling at God, questioning why everything was falling apart. Why, after everything, did it feel like I was losing it all? The doubts and fears began to eat away at me until there was nothing left but the darkness.

And in the middle of that darkness, I made a choice. I cheated on Phill. It wasn't some mistake or moment of weakness. It was intentional, deliberate. I was drowning, and for the first time, someone saw me. He had been there, this family friend, watching the fights, the lies, the drinking. He saw what was happening, and in those moments, I felt free. I felt seen in a way that I hadn't in years. I didn't feel like I was drowning anymore.

It wasn't about love. It wasn't about revenge. It was about liberation. It was about finally letting go of the weight that had been crushing me for years. For the first time, I wasn't thinking about anyone else—about Jr., or Phill, or my family. I was thinking about me. And it felt good. It felt like I had finally broken free from the chains that had been binding me.

But freedom came with a price. When the dust settled and I came back to reality, I realized what I had done. I had betrayed Phill, I had betrayed myself, and I had shattered the life we had built. Fourteen years, my family, everything we had—none of it mattered anymore. In that moment of clarity, I packed a bag, and I left.

I didn't look back.

What I didn't realize then, though, was that leaving wasn't just an escape. It was a death. A death to the person I had been, the person who had been defined by everyone else's expectations, everyone else's needs. I had to die to myself, to the version of me that was constantly in survival mode, to the person who had buried her own pain to keep everyone else together.

This was my moment of repentance—not just in the spiritual sense, but in the deepest, most personal way. I had to face the consequences of my choices, of my sins, of the ways I had hurt myself and others. I had to face God and ask for forgiveness—not just for cheating, but for losing myself along the way. I had to ask for the strength to become someone new, someone who could live in truth, even when that truth was painful.

Phill's death was more than the loss of a person; it was the end of a chapter in my life. The end of who I had been and the beginning of someone new. Someone who had died to herself and was now learning what it meant to live again, this time with a heart of repentance and a spirit ready to rebuild.

The storm had passed, and in its wake, there was devastation. But there was also hope. Hope that from the ashes, something new could rise. And for the first time in a long time, I believed that it could.

WAKING UP ON SEPTEMBER 19TH

September 19, 2018, 10:36 a.m. The phone buzzed, startling me awake. I rubbed my eyes, disoriented. Ninety-two missed calls. A wave of dread crashed over me as I scrolled through the names—family, friends, even people I hadn't spoken to in months. My phone had been off after a fight with Phill earlier that night. That fight had spiraled into another argument with Dolla, the man I was with in Vegas. Yes, Dolla. A name I hadn't mentioned before because he represented a chapter of my life that I wasn't proud of.

When I left Phill, I left with a couple and their friend Dolla —a pimp. I had thrown myself into a situationship that was all too familiar, even though I had vowed to leave my old ways behind. But Vegas has a way of pulling you into its depths. It's why I call it Babylon—no nature, no real water source, just a desert hiding secrets under layers of glitter and neon lights. I had been around working girls before, even been a madam in the past. It felt like I had regressed, not grown, despite my intentions of shedding the old me.

Phill had no idea what was happening. He didn't see the cheating or me leaving for Vegas coming. The weight loss, my new image—it made him think the worst. His mind spun out of control, convinced I had been kidnapped or was selling myself. I could hear it in the voicemails he left, especially the one with that song—I still see your shadows in my room. I couldn't shake the memory of it.

But the call that changed everything came from Sherri, a mutual friend who had been close to both Phill and me. When I finally answered the phone, her voice trembled on the other end.

"Nana, are you sitting down? I need to tell you something. No one wants me to tell you…"

There was a pause. I braced myself.

"Phill died."

My heart stopped. I couldn't process the words. Phill died. It echoed in my mind, over and over. I screamed, I cried, but nothing seemed real. Twenty-eight days after I left, twenty-eight days of fights, confusion, and distance—Phill was gone. He had been drinking and driving, and we had argued just minutes before his death. I hadn't even thought about turning my phone back on until it was too late. Now, I was drowning in the what-ifs and the guilt.

Phill Jr. was the first person that came to my mind—his son, the boy who had tried so hard to get his father's attention. Then came thoughts of his daughter, his wife, his friends… so many people who were going to be devastated. I had caused chaos when I left, but this was something I could never have prepared for. And the one thing that kept replaying in my mind? No one wanted me to know.

It became clear that the circle of friends we had once shared was gone. They didn't want me at the funeral or the memorial. I had lost everything in a flash. And while some tried to comfort me, telling me I should still go, I knew deep down that I wasn't welcome. Fourteen years of my life had been intertwined with Phill's, and it felt like that chapter had been erased, as if I had never existed. Even the ability to have children with him had been taken from me. I had lost my second fallopian tube in another ectopic pregnancy, resulting in a partial hysterectomy. The grief of that loss was wrapped up in the grief of losing him.

There was going to be a candlelight vigil in Vegas at Desert Breeze Park, where he had met his wife while playing basketball. Two nights before the vigil, my best friend called me. We hadn't spoken in a while—one of those breaks we often took—but she came immediately when she found out. Just like she always did. She was my constant, my anchor, even though our first encounter had been as enemies. Now, we were inseparable, and she shared motherhood with me in ways I couldn't have imagined.

I didn't want to go to the vigil. Not because of fear or guilt, but out of love. This wasn't about me; it was about Phill, and I wanted to respect the space for his family to grieve. I stood at a distance, watching the people I once knew gather to mourn him. I saw a few familiar faces, caught a few glares, but I also saw his children and the women who had brought him the greatest joy. That was enough for me —it gave me the closure I needed.

Still, the pain was raw. I thought about everything Phill represented in my life—love, struggle, and the loss that had marked so many of our years together. His death, like his life, was a reminder of the things I couldn't change: the infertility, the mistakes, the years spent in survival mode. But I was also reminded of the love that existed between us and the fact that no matter how things ended, Phill was a part of me that I could never erase.

My mom brought balloons and flowers, giving them to Phill's kids, and I was grateful for her support. She, along with my best friend, helped me through those dark days. The grief felt endless, but so did their love.

Phill's death marked the end of an era—fourteen years of love, loss, and everything in between. But it also marked the beginning of something new, even though I couldn't see it at the time. I had spent my entire adult life with him, and now I had to figure out who I was without him. The journey was far from over, but I knew one thing for certain: no one could ever take away what we had or the lessons I had learned from loving and losing him.

Journal Entry Exercise: Coping with Loss and Grief

Introduction: Grief is a deeply personal and often overwhelming emotion, but writing can be a powerful tool for processing the complex feelings that come with loss. In this exercise, we will reflect on the themes of Chapter 15—loss, guilt, isolation, and finding closure in unexpected ways. This exercise is designed to help you navigate your own grief and find moments of peace and healing.

Instructions:

Find a quiet, comfortable space where you can focus. Take a few deep breaths, and allow yourself to feel whatever emotions come up. Remember, there are no right or wrong answers in this exercise—this is your time to process and reflect.

Step 1: Acknowledge Your Loss

1. Begin by writing about the loss you are grieving. This could be the loss of a person, a relationship, a part of yourself, or even a dream.

Prompt:

"The loss I am grieving is… (write about the person or situation you have lost, including how they/it made you feel when they were present in your life)."

Take your time here. Describe your emotions honestly, even if they are conflicted. Sometimes grief comes with guilt, relief, confusion, or anger. It's important to give space to all these emotions.

____

____

____

____

____

____

Step 2: The What-Ifs and Guilt

Loss often leaves us with questions and "what-ifs." It's common to feel guilt, regret, or wonder if things could have turned out differently. Let's explore that without judgment.

Prompt:

"The thoughts that keep replaying in my mind are… (write about any guilt, regrets, or unanswered questions you have. It could be something you wish you had said or done differently)."

Now, take a moment to write a letter of forgiveness to yourself. Let go of the idea that you could have controlled everything. Grief is unpredictable, and sometimes things happen outside of our power.

Prompt:

"I forgive myself for... (write about the things you're holding onto that you need to release)."

Step 3: Finding the Silver Lining

Even in the darkest moments of grief, there can be unexpected lessons or gifts. Reflect on how this loss, while painful, may have changed you or brought you closer to something deeper.

Prompt:

"Through this loss, I have learned... (write about the insights, strength, or unexpected growth you have found through grieving, even if it feels small)."

Step 4: Closure and Release

1. Closure doesn't mean forgetting; it means finding peace. Visualize yourself sitting down with the person or situation you've lost. Imagine what you would say to them if you had the chance for one last conversation.

Prompt:

"If I could speak to you now, I would say... (write as if you are having a final conversation, expressing anything you feel is unresolved or that you wish you could have said)."

After you finish, take a moment to reflect on what closure looks like for you. What does it feel like to release some of the pain or confusion you've been carrying?

____

____

____

____

____

____

Step 5: Moving Forward with Grace

Grief doesn't disappear, but we can learn to carry it more gently over time. Think about one small step you can take to move forward in your healing.

Prompt:

"One way I can honor my loss and still move forward is… (write about a small, manageable step you can take to honor the person or situation while also focusing on your own healing and growth)."

____

____

____

____

Closing Reflection:

Take a deep breath and reflect on what you've written. Grief is not linear, and it's okay to have good days and bad days. Be gentle with yourself as you move forward. Healing comes in waves, and it's important to give yourself time and space to feel.

____

____

____

____

____

You can return to this journal exercise anytime the weight of loss feels too heavy or when you need to process the complex emotions that come with grief. Let writing be your tool for release, reflection, and, eventually, healing.

THE SIGN AND THE YOGA DUDE IN THE RANGE ROVER

Living with my parents after everything fell apart was like sitting in a pressure cooker, and the heat just kept rising. They hated their situation, and honestly, I wasn't thrilled about it either. Every argument, every complaint—it felt like their dissatisfaction was feeding my own darkness. I was spiraling, asking myself over and over, "If they hadn't moved in with us, would I have left Phill?" I started questioning everything. Maybe it was all just bad timing, or maybe my so-called "brightest days" were a lie. I had been basing so much on how I looked after losing all that weight, but now? Now nothing mattered.

Each morning, I woke up with the same thought: I don't want to do this anymore. I prayed that I wouldn't wake up the next day. I started imagining myself just falling asleep and slipping away for good. The darkness crept in until, one day, I tried to make that a reality. I thought about ending it. But if there's one thing my family history taught me, it's this: don't tell the doctors what you're planning. You end up under their thumb, another number in the system. It felt like survival was just another form of control, and I wanted out.

But, of course, after the attempt, life didn't get easier. I walked back into the chaos of my parents fighting over money, the usual routine of blame and frustration. That's when something inside me snapped. I grabbed a marker, some cardboard, and I made a sign. A real, raw, "I'm done" kind of sign. I took it to the streets, sat outside the Walmart in Centennial, and poured my soul onto that piece of cardboard. I didn't even care what people thought. I just sat there and cried, letting the universe know how broken I felt.

And the weirdest part? People gave me money. For a week straight, I sat on that corner, and I made enough to help my parents pay rent. It wasn't a solution, but it was something.

On the last day, I was at a different corner and needed to use the bathroom, so I headed to the nearest gas station. Out of nowhere, a Range Rover pulled up beside me. My first thought? Great. Another guy trying to "help" me. In Vegas, I had seen it all—men preying on the weak, acting like they were offering help, but we all knew what they really wanted.

But this wasn't that. A yoga-looking guy stepped out. I swear, he was so short, I thought a kid had stolen his mom's car. His head barely cleared the steering wheel, and the second he started talking, I knew he wasn't trying to hit on me. He wasn't my type, and I definitely wasn't his.

With a Rolex glinting off his wrist, he leaned out of the window and asked, "What's that you're holding?"

I showed him the sign, still half-expecting some weird comment.

"I just left yoga and feel centered with spirit," he said, sounding like a walking meditation app.

Then he surprised me. "You're having a hard time," he said, genuine concern in his voice.

No kidding.

He handed me a business card and said, "I'll see you tomorrow at 7 a.m. My office is right next door." And then he just drove off, like some kind of spiritual Uber driver.

For reasons I still can't explain, I went home, packed my stuff, and woke up early the next morning. I wasn't sure what I was walking into, but something about his offer felt...different. When I got to his office, it wasn't at all what I expected. This wasn't some corporate stiff job. It was a small energy brokerage, and he was offering me a commission-based sales job. The place was a total YouTuber's dream—catered meals, weed on deck, and a room with video games and a pool table. I wasn't stupid; I knew how to hustle. The commission was $1,700 a pop, no cap on earnings, and he even threw in perks like trips and cars.

So, what did I do? I went to work. First day, five sales, $5,000 in my pocket. Just like that. Suddenly, I wasn't praying to die anymore. I was distracted by the money, and for the first time in what felt like forever, I was happy.

But here's the thing: my happiness was wrapped up in cash. I wasn't healed; I was just distracted. It didn't take long to realize that. Still, I couldn't deny it—I felt alive again, even if it was just the adrenaline rush of the hustle. Life has a funny way of throwing you curveballs. One minute, you're crying on a street corner with a sign, and the next, you're rolling in cash, thanks to a yoga dude in a Range Rover.

Who knew the universe had that kind of sense of humor?

I WANT MY LIFE BACK

It became clear to me that it was never about money. Life is far too complex to be reduced to mere currency. After all, money is just paper—it lost much of its value back in 1971, and as of 2024, 159 countries have completely dropped the American dollar. This truth hit me hard, like a slap to the face, forcing me to confront a deeper reality. Once again, I found myself slipping into that dark, cold, and familiar place. I still never turned to drugs, but I sat directly in the numbness, surrounded by others who felt the same, except for my brother. Even he seemed distant, barely knowing me anymore.

The haunting memories of my 14-year relationship with Phill weighed on me heavily. It was never an on-again, off-again fling; we lived together, worked together, and shared everything. Those who knew us understood the depth of our bond. But as the money poured in, I found myself drowning deeper. I had resources, yet I left my parents and allowed Dolla to stay behind. That's when I realized things had truly changed. My parents had always opened their door to anyone—my cousins, neighborhood kids, and other family members—but now I was gone, and Dolla was still there.

Looking back, I owe my family and my best friend a huge apology. What was I thinking? I barely knew Dolla, and yet I left him in their home, putting them in a situation they never asked for. Yes, we were all losing ourselves during that time, but I know there will be consequences for my choices.

Then came the darkest moment: another suicide attempt. This time, I was gone for 1 minute and 32 seconds. When I woke up, I had been stripped of everything—my wig, my clothes, my phone. I was under evaluation, and what felt like six months turned out to be only three, maybe four. During that time, I found a strange kind of comfort in talking about what I had been through, letting it all out. Yet the way I was handled—labeled, documented, and prescribed medication—was traumatizing in its own way. It felt like dying all over again, and worse, because we are not meant to die. We are made to live long, meaningful lives, like those of Noah, who lived for over 400 years. Even after death, the spirit lives on. Yet, here we are, taught to kill ourselves by not fulfilling our true purpose—God's purpose.

I could have been lost in that system forever, trapped by labels and prescriptions. But through prayer and the protection of my energies, I was given another chance. In what felt like divine intervention, my work, after adding me to the company's board, asked me to relocate. I was headed to Medellín, Colombia. It was another hand dealt in life, another opportunity for a new chapter.

VIVA LA COLOMBIA

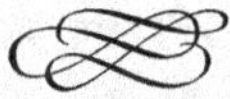

Colombia will forever be my home. I absolutely loved it—full of culture, music, laughter, and incredible food. Even what it lacked became a source of comfort. The absence of emotional attachment, the unfamiliarity, and the inability to easily communicate in English all felt like a release. And yes, I loved the menthol cigarettes—I am a smoker. I loved every bit of it.

Being so far away wasn't just comforting; it was a way to truly unravel. A space to surrender, to get to know myself. I learned about energy, how powerful it is, and how much love can be felt. Just like faith, it's not about what you hear or see, but how it makes you feel. Vibrating in the frequency of love is like knowing gold, and that's exactly what it felt like.

After three months of work drama, I decided to move out of Poblado, where the Americans and wealthy expats lived for a good time. Instead, I moved in with what felt like a family—a Colombian family. That was the best experience: no hot water, no tech conveniences, and half the roof of the house missing. It was amazing.

Where I'm from in California, the wealthy live in the hills. But in Medellin, the worse the neighborhood, the higher up you lived. And the views? They were breathtaking. I can't even explain the energy of Colombia—it felt like home, even more than home ever did.

I felt protected, loved, and the people around me—most of whom I couldn't even speak the same language with—communicated through energy. It was like we were all connected through memories and feelings, and that was enough.

The food was fresh, the music lifted you up, and there were endless days of laughter. Not once did I have to focus on finding peace; it just was. And I realized why—there were no emotional triggers, no attachments. That's why it felt like peace.

TRIGGERED AGAIN!

Back in Vegas, what was supposed to be a quick three-month stay before heading back to Colombia turned into something else entirely. I had to wait on my work visa, so I was preparing to go back and forth. The contract in Colombia was for five years, and I was genuinely looking forward to it. But during that time, Dolla had moved out of my parents' place and into my best friend Kapua's home. I never admitted it to her, but I had orchestrated that situation, and for that, I owe her an apology. She had kids, and honestly, I barely knew Dolla. But when you're hurt, you sometimes act out of that pain and unintentionally drag others into it.

I lacked accountability for that and, in doing so, caused trauma. We must be better to ourselves so we don't hurt those around us. I thought Dolla's stay at my parents' place wouldn't last long, but it did. My dad was mentally exhausted by that point, or maybe he was trying to be there for me in ways he hadn't before. I think he carried guilt over some things he'd said about Phill, knowing how much Phill loved me. His allowing Dolla to stay might have been an unnoticed attempt to show me love, and in my own way, I might have hurt my dad in return by not recognizing that.

As expected, Kapua wasn't having it. She's worked her ass off for years and wasn't about to put up with someone who just smoked, drank, and played video games all day. Like I thought, Dolla was gone soon after. And of course, as soon as I landed in Vegas, I was right back with Kapua.

A couple of months passed, and one day, while picking up her daughter's friend from the airport, I was introduced to a man from Israel. Odd as it might sound, we hit it off immediately. Not in a romantic way, but we had a lot in common despite coming from completely different walks of life.

Four months in, he asked me to marry him. His reason was honest and spiritual—something that struck a chord with me. At first, I said no. It didn't seem possible; I mean, I was a convinced lesbian, had fallen in love with Phill, and then there was Dolla. No, it couldn't work. But that night, something strange happened. Phill came to me for the first time since his passing. He told me, "You've been asking for this, and you'd be dumb not to take it."

I sat with that for what felt like forever. Finally, I called him back, and we met for lunch at Panera Bread in South

Vegas. We talked about purpose, about life, and about what this marriage would mean. I was still stuck in my no—until I asked one question. "What would my last name be?"

He said, "Barshalom."

"And what does that mean? English, please."

He smiled and said, "God's peace."

Suddenly, it hit me like a tidal wave. I had forgotten an important part of my journey—those triggers are real. One word, one memory, and everything floods back. I had done an ayahuasca ceremony and asked for peace—God's peace. And here it was, literally being offered to me. That sealed it for me. I said yes.

A JOURNEY OF GROWTH AND SECOND CHANCES

Life started to flow again in ways I hadn't expected. My marriage with Eran wasn't traditional by any means. It was a spiritual alignment, something divinely timed and deeply rooted in the healing I experienced in Colombia. That part of my journey deserves its own story, its own book, because the ceremony we went through was life-changing. Eran had opportunities in Oregon and soon left to pursue them, while I was planning to return to Colombia. Our connection wasn't bound by the usual expectations of marriage—it was based on understanding, trust, and the lessons we both needed at the time. The timing was perfect, as it brought essential growth into my life.

As I stayed behind, I found myself spending more time with Kapua, my best friend who had always been my grounding force. Around the same time, I had just earned an Audi after being the top sales rep for six months straight while also opening an office in Colombia. It felt like everything I had worked for was finally paying off, and I was proud of that. But driving—well, that wasn't something I'd embraced, especially after Phill. He had always been the one behind the wheel, and I never really took that space back for myself until now.

I decided to show off the new car and headed over to Kapua's house. Her man had a friend over—Ronte, a Westside Blood, who caught my attention right away. He was familiar, comforting even, and the evening quickly felt like an impromptu double date. Kapua and I were cooking, the guys were gaming, and the kids were running around. As the night went on, the idea of driving home in the dark didn't feel right, so I handed Ronte the keys and invited him along for the ride.

What started as a casual connection turned into something more. Ronte and I ended up spending two years together. He had his ways—he was a dealer, a ladies' man, and there were definitely other women involved. But for some reason, I stayed focused on my own path. I was working long hours—12-hour days, six days a week—so I wasn't around much anyway. He had the space to live his life, and I lived mine. It wasn't perfect, but it was what it was.

Then COVID hit, and everything shifted. Suddenly, it was just us, stuck in this new reality where scarcity and uncertainty shaped our dynamic. Yet, in those challenging times, I saw a different side of him. Ronte is a beautiful soul—caring, soft, funny, and a true momma's boy. His love for his mother was unmatched, and he was hardworking. But the world we lived in wasn't kind to people like him, and I could see how it wore on him.

I had planned to return to Colombia, but the pandemic stopped that from happening. So I thought, maybe we could make it work—maybe this was the time to build something more. But after two years together, I wasn't sure if what we had gone through was enough to build a future on. Still, I knew how much an environmental change could help, because it had done wonders for me in the past. So I took a chance. We packed up and left Vegas, hoping that Colorado would offer the fresh start we both needed.

Moving to Colorado felt like the right decision. I hoped that by removing Ronte from his old environment, he would find the space to heal and grow, just like I had when I left for Colombia. I knew it wasn't going to be easy, but I also knew that sometimes, the biggest transformations happen when you step away from the familiar and take that leap into the unknown. And that's exactly what we did.

FLOURISHING TOGETHER IN COLORADO

The decision to move to Colorado with Ronte was one of uncertainty and risk. After everything we had been through—both individually and as a couple—I wasn't sure what this next chapter held. But from the moment we arrived, something shifted. It was as if Colorado welcomed us with open arms, offering not just a fresh start but a place for us to truly thrive.

We both found good-paying jobs almost immediately, and that sense of financial stability brought us peace. We weren't just surviving anymore; we were building a life together. The work allowed us to focus on healing, both personally and as a couple. We committed to growth every chance we had, taking time to understand ourselves and each other in ways we hadn't before. Our healing journey became intertwined, and soon we were flourishing in ways I hadn't imagined.

We quickly became more than just a couple going through the motions of daily life. We started hosting our own events, something I had never expected. It wasn't just about finding ways to heal ourselves; we wanted to give back, to create spaces where others could heal too. These events became a creative outlet for both of us. We'd spend nights talking, bouncing ideas off one another, and dreaming big. It was like we had become partners not only in love but also in purpose. Each event felt like a reflection of the journey we were on, and we were doing it together.

The people around us didn't understand how we worked so well. On the surface, we seemed too different, too mismatched. They didn't expect us to click the way we did, and I'll admit, at first, I didn't either. But as we spent more time together, I realized that our differences were what made us work. It wasn't just love; it was the kind of connection where you gain a best friend while falling in love. There's something powerful about being seen for who you really are and having that person stand beside you through it all.

In Colorado, we weren't just healing the past—we were creating something new. Our relationship wasn't about fixing what was broken; it was about building something stronger than either of us had before. The more we invested in each other and our shared vision, the more I realized that we had been brought together for a reason. Our paths had crossed at the right time, and our connection deepened with every step we took.

Colorado became a place of transformation. The mountains, the fresh air, the new opportunities—it all felt like a metaphor for what was happening between us. We were rising, growing, becoming the people we were meant to be. Our love wasn't just about passion; it was about partnership, about finding someone who not only understood your journey but wanted to walk beside you in theirs.

Together, we found a rhythm, a balance that allowed us both to shine. The world saw us as two different people, but we knew that our differences were our strengths. We had become more than just two people in love. We were a team, a force, and the life we were building was proof that sometimes, when you least expect it, everything comes together exactly as it's supposed to.

Colorado wasn't just a change of scenery—it was the place where we found ourselves, and each other, in ways we never could have imagined.

THE LAST BREATH OF A LIFETIME

April 18th, 2022, is a day I will never forget. It was the day I got the call. My father had lost oxygen for more than 10 minutes, and the doctors said he wouldn't make it out of ICU. The weight of that news hit me like a freight train. I was at the 420 event in downtown Denver with Ronte, celebrating a day my dad would have appreciated. He was a lifetime toker, after all. This year, we were listening to local baddie Rachel Bailey, alongside legends like E-40 and Lil Jon. I could feel my dad's spirit in the music, the energy, and the haze that filled the air.

Instead of being weighed down by the looming grief, I chose to enjoy the rest of the evening. It felt like something my dad would've wanted. A lifetime of lessons flowed through me as I prepared for what would come next. The very next day, I was on a plane to Vegas, the city that raised me. The city that taught me so much about sin, survival, and resilience. And now, it was the city where I would say goodbye.

Vegas has always felt like Babylon to me, with its overwhelming energy—a place where the mafia, the hustle, and the games of life seemed to converge. It wasn't just the COPD that took my dad—it was the consumption of fear and trauma that wore him down. He despised Vegas, hated its lack of community, its coldness. He often told me how this city, and this world, was playing a deadly game with humanity, a chess match where we were the pawns. My dad had lived in that game for 55 years, and it had worn him out.

I've often wondered if it wasn't his disease that took him, but the weight of the world. The suffocating feeling of watching everything unravel while you're powerless to change it. He lived a life of suffering, unable to sit back and do nothing, but also unsure how to stop the cycle. In his way, he was trying to teach me that this world will always test us, push us, break us—but in those moments, we have to decide what kind of game we are playing.

Our relationship had been distant for years, but in his death, life started making more sense. My dad had been preparing me for this moment, giving me the strength to let go of all the pain I once blamed on him. In losing him, I gained a deeper understanding. One of the biggest roles of our parents is to guide us back to our heavenly Father. Through their mistakes, through their love, through their absence, they shape the paths we walk.

Now, at 36, I see my life for what it is: a journey of accountability, love, and healing. The movements I have started, the fights I have chosen, all come from that same place —the desire to end the suffering I've seen all my life. Whether it was the physical and emotional abuse I endured, the rape, the infertility, or the loss of love, every wound has become a piece of my armor. Every scar is a reminder of who I am and where I've been. And every time life reminds me of those wounds, I find strength in the beauty that lies within the pain.

I've always believed that we can't run from our pain. We can't pretend it doesn't exist. But what we can do is turn it into something meaningful. We can use it to find our way back to ourselves, back to our truth, back to God. Authentic. Whole. In His image.

I'm a widow. A woman who has survived infertility. A girl who was raised in love, even through pain. My father's death was not the end of the story. It was just the next chapter, the next lesson. He was a man who loved deeply, who carried the weight of the world on his shoulders. And in his passing, he set me free to live the life I was meant to live.

This is not the end. It is only the beginning.

In the game of life, we will all face moments of loss, moments of pain, moments where it feels like the world is closing in on us. But those moments are where we find the deepest lessons, where we discover who we really are. We are not just players in a game—we are the storytellers, the creators, the ones who have the power to change the narrative.

And with every step forward, I will continue to fight—to end the fight of human suffering, to curate safe spaces for healing, for trauma to be acknowledged, for accountability to lead the way. My father may be gone, but his legacy lives on in me. The strength, the fire, the desire to live a life of purpose.

I will continue telling my story, because it matters. And so does yours.

Journal Exercise: Embracing Your Story and Healing Through Confidence

This exercise is designed to help you reflect on your personal journey, acknowledge the healing you've experienced, and build confidence in sharing your story. As you journal, embrace honesty and self-compassion, allowing yourself to fully connect with your thoughts and feelings.

Step 1: Reflect on Your Healing Journey

Begin by taking a few deep breaths, centering yourself in the present moment. When you're ready, answer the following questions:

- What have been the key moments of healing in your life? (Think about experiences that helped you grow emotionally, spiritually, or physically.)

- Who or what played a significant role in your healing process?
- How did these moments change the way you view yourself and the world around you?

Journal Prompt:

Describe a healing experience that has had a lasting impact on your life. What did this healing reveal about your inner strength? How did it shift your perspective on your journey?

____

____

____

____

____

Step 2: Reclaiming Your Narrative

Your story is a powerful tool for both personal growth and inspiring others. Reflect on your journey and the lessons you've learned:

- What is the most important lesson you've learned from your experiences?
- How have your challenges shaped who you are today?

- What do you want others to understand about your journey?

Journal Prompt:

Write about a challenge or obstacle you've overcome that has become a central part of your story. How did this experience make you stronger? How do you feel now about telling others about it?

____

____

____

____

____

Step 3: Building Confidence in Telling Your Story

Sharing your story requires vulnerability but can also be deeply empowering. Take a moment to explore how confident you feel about sharing your story with others.

- What fears or doubts do you have about telling your story?
- What would it feel like to fully embrace your story and share it with confidence?
- How can sharing your story help others who may be going through similar experiences?

Journal Prompt:

Imagine you are about to tell your story to a close friend or a group of supportive people. How do you feel as you begin? What emotions come up as you speak your truth? Write about how it feels to confidently share your story, knowing that it holds value for others.

____

____

____

____

____

____

Step 4: Affirming Your Power

End the exercise by affirming the power of your story and your place in the world.

Journal Prompt:

Write an affirmation or statement that captures your confidence in telling your story. For example: "I am proud of my journey, and my story holds the power to inspire healing and change in others."

Feel free to return to this exercise whenever you need to reconnect with your strength and the significance of your story. You hold a unique and beautiful perspective, and by sharing it, you contribute to the healing of others as well as yourself.